My Safe Community

Colleen Hord

ROURKE
PUBLISHING
www.rourkepublishing.com

www.rourkepublishing.com

PHOTO CREDITS: Cover: © Goldenkb; Title Page © Gregory Johnston; Page 3 © laflor; Page 5 © manley099; Page 7 © Benjamin F. Haith; Page 9, 16 © jacomstephens; Page 11 © kozmoat98; Page 13 © monkeybusinessimages; Page 15 © Shaun Lowe; Page 17 © WomanRay; Page 18 © asiseeit; Page 19 © iofoto; Page 20 © Damian Dovarganes   AP. 101021026659; Page 21 © shironosov

Edited by Meg Greve

Cover design by Tara Ramo
Interior design by Renee Brady

Library of Congress Cataloging-in-Publication Data

Hord, Colleen
 My Safe Community / Colleen Hord.
    p. cm. -- (Little World Social Studies)
 Includes bibliographical references and index.
 ISBN 978-1-61741-795-5 (hard cover) (alk. paper)
 ISBN 978-1-61741-997-3 (soft cover)
 Library of Congress Control Number: 2011925065

Rourke Publishing
Printed in the United States of America, North Mankato, Minnesota
060711
060711CL

www.rourkepublishing.com - rourke@rourkepublishing.com
Post Office Box 643328 Vero Beach, Florida 32964

Living in a safe **community** is important to everyone.

You want to be safe whether you are shopping, playing at the park, or walking to school.

Sometimes the adults in a community **elect** leaders who make decisions that keep you safe.

A ballot is a way of voting.

The **mayor** and **city council** members are community leaders who are elected. They work with other community workers.

The **sanitation workers** help the mayor keep the town clean by collecting garbage and keeping people safe from germs.

The people on the city council listen to the people who live in the community so they know when a new park or stop sign is needed.

Firefighters teach you about fire safety and help those who are in an accident until an ambulance arrives.

Signs tell us community safety rules. Police officers keep you safe by making sure everyone follows the rules.

Many people work to keep you safe at school. The crossing guards keep you safe when you are walking to school.

Teachers help keep you safe by practicing fire, tornado, and earthquake **drills**.

We love our safe community!

Picture Glossary

 **city council** (CIT-ee KOUN-suhl): A group of people chosen to look after the interests of a city or town.

 **community** (Kuh-MYOO-nuh-tee): A place where a group of people live, work, and care for each other.

 **drills** (DRILLZ): Practicing what to do in case of an emergency.

elect (i-LEKT): To choose someone by voting for them.

mayor (MAY- ur): The leader of a town or city.

sanitation workers (san-uh-TAY-shun WUR-kurs): The people who pick up garbage and take it away.

Index

Websites

www.kids.gov

www.brainpopjr.com/socialstudies/communities/

www.firesafety.gov/kids

About the Author

Colleen Hord lives on a small farm with her husband, llamas, chickens, and cats. She enjoys kayaking, camping, walking on the beach, and reading to her grandchildren.